FANS

ON

FIRE!

How to Skyrocket Your Leads, Sales, and Reputation with the Most Trusted Form of Marketing

Written By: Tom Kenemore

www.TomKenemore.com

Lake Effect
Media

Publishing services provided by:

 **Archangel Ink**

ISBN-13: 978-1533320254
ISBN: 153332025X

Disclaimer:

The information in this book is for general reference and educational purposes only. This publication is not intended to provide tailored recommendations nor is it a basis for actions without careful analysis and due diligence. The strategies in this book may not be suitable for every individual or business. Neither the author nor the publisher is liable for any actions promoted or caused by the information presented in this book. Any views expressed herein are those of the author and do not represent the views of others. Any perceived slight of any individual or organization is purely unintentional.

Lead Your Market With The Best Marketing Money Can't Buy – Authentic Online Reviews!

- Do you want to have the best reputation in your local market?

- Do you want more leads and sales for your business without increasing your budget?

- Are negative online reviews about your business, product or service pissing you off?

- Do you want to earn the customer service awards your competition has won?

Most businesses are missing a HUGE opportunity to leverage their existing happy customer's goodwill into FREE marketing! Through a simple, yet unconventional strategy, this book will show you:

- How to build a continuous source of free, new leads for your business.

- How to gate or control which customers will write online reviews for you.

- How to build or rebuild your online reputation (your social proof) and your national and local search engine optimization (SEO) with online reviews.

- What the most popular review websites are and how to find the review websites specific to your industry.

- How to leverage your new and existing positive customer reviews for maximum benefit.

- How some of the most popular Internet review websites work.

- How to handle negative and fake reviews about your product, service or company.

- How to handle a complaining customer.

- BONUS: Online Review Marketing Quick Start Guide & 12 email, letter, webpage templates and more!

All with full integrity . . . using only legitimate strategies . . . only real customers and real reviews! No black hat techniques, unethical reputation management firms, or fake reviews allowed!

So join over 5000 successful students that have already learned and applied my online review strategies that I call "Fans on Fire!"

Your Free Gifts

Thank you for purchasing this book! Get a jump start to leveraging your online reviews!

Download your copy of my FREE Online Review Marketing Quick Start Guide & 12 email, letter, webpage templates and more!

Just follow the link below to claim your free gifts!

http://tomkenemore.com/firebonuses

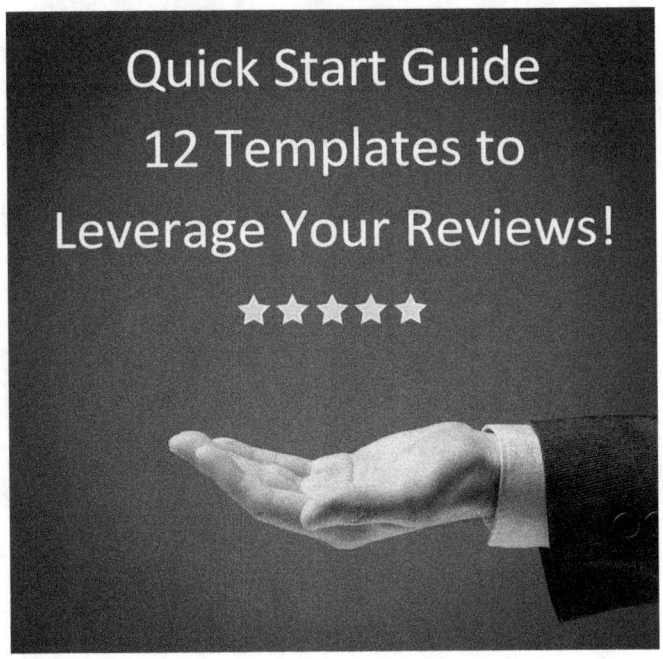

Contents

Chapter 1

Introduction

"Your happy clients and customers are your most valuable asset!"

– Tom Kenemore

IS THIS BOOK FOR YOU?

Well do any of these statements fit you?

- You want more leads for your business but don't have or don't want to increase the budget for more advertising.
- Negative online reviews about your business, product or service are pissing you off!
- You want to earn the customer service awards your competition has won.
- You want the reputation of being an industry leader in your market.

So how can you make one or more of those statements a reality? By implementing a strategy I developed called Fans on Fire – Leveraged online reviews!

Whether you are thinking of starting a business or you are a seasoned, long time entrepreneur, managing and leveraging your customers' online reviews are vital to your business's success! In the last few years online reviews on websites, search engines and social media have exploded across the Internet. These online reviews are boldly featured on Yelp, Google, Yahoo, Bing, Facebook and so many more Internet properties.

Ask yourself this question. What did you do before the last time you made a purchase? Odds are that you looked for online reviews of the product or service and the company (or both) before you made a purchasing decision. According to a survey by Dimensional Research, 90% or 9 out of 10 customers claimed positive reviews influenced their purchasing decision. On the flip side, 86% of those surveyed said their buying decision was influenced by negative online reviews! Now that should either scare you or excite you!

I love marketing. Marketing is one of my passions! But do you know what I love more than marketing? **_FREE_** marketing! Few if any free marketing efforts can beat the power of legitimate online reviews. Your business's online reputation is either an asset or a liability. These days a future potential customer only has to hit a few keystrokes to find out what your past customers are saying about you. And even if your prospects don't search out your reviews, they will likely be served up on a platter to your prospects by Google and many search engines.

Great Internet marketing is all about stellar content and natural, organic search engine optimization. Search engines like Google love online reviews for their content! The more positive reviews the better! Plus each review website is another potential page 1 listing for you on Google. Would you like 2, 3 or 4 page one listings on Google? I'll show you how with these strategies. So what is your process for getting online reviews? If you don't have one . . . you really need to read this book! If your current online review process is just a page on your website or an email or letter asking your customers to review you online, that is a great start, but you are missing out! This book will show you a simple system for managing your online reviews and then leveraging them for their maximum marketing benefit.

STOP STRUGGLING

Look, haven't you struggled with your online reputation long enough? Maybe you are less excited about the marketing part of online reviews and really just want to clean up your online reputation. If you've been in business for a while like me, I'm sure you have been frustrated at one point or another with all of the online review websites. Maybe you don't feel like you have any control over who posts a review or not.

There are few things more disappointing than having spent years creating and refining a business you believe will truly help people, only to have an angry customer rip it down online from one bad experience! Or what's worse is if it wasn't even a real customer, but a spammer writing you a fake bad review online. I'm not going to debate whether these online review websites are fair or not, because like it or not, online reviews are here to stay and will likely become even more important to your business in the future.

When I had my wedding DJ company, one of our top lead sources was prospects from online review websites. I spent years developing this system and carefully leveraging our online review profiles. Besides gathering hundreds of awesome online reviews, we won 11 state wedding awards. But it even got better! We also received a brand new national wedding award from TheKnot.com! We were one of just 331 of all wedding related companies in the entire United States to receive this award and we were interviewed by 2 local TV stations. Needless to say, it was great publicity and all because of working this system and providing a great service.

WILL THIS WORK IN MY BUSINESS?

As business owners, we need to take control of our business's destiny! I wrote this book so business owners and managers everywhere can take control of their online reputations and maximize their marketing potential. Through trial and error and over 25 years of my own small business experience, I've carefully developed the Fans on Fire system. I want every business owner or manager to be able to master their online reputations and leverage them to the max!

So will this Fans on Fire system work in my business or industry? If you or your business can be rated on any online review website, then it will work in your business. If you are in a competitive industry, great online reviews are not just nice to have, they are a requirement! You will need to have a bunch of them just to be on an even playing field with your competition.

Now try this. Pretend to be a potential customer for *YOUR* business. Type in a Google search box, your business name followed by the word "reviews"...Gulp! Did you do it or were you too afraid of what might come up? If you are not happy with the results of this search, what can you do? A lot actually! In just the first few chapters of this book, you'll learn how to start improving your online reputation! In this book you'll learn why online reviews are critical for attracting more clients and sales. I'll show you what review websites all businesses should target and how to find the review websites that are specific to your industry. I'll cover how to get your customers to give you those awesome reviews and then how to leverage them for their maximum positive impact.

Plus if you've gotten negative reviews in the past, I'll show you how to bury those with positive reviews and lessen their impact on your business. With this book you'll also get all the email, letter and webpage templates that you need. These templates are ready to go, just add your specific business text updates. I'll walk you through, step by step, from getting the initial review from your clients to getting your clients to post them to the top online review websites. But we won't stop there; I'll show you how to leverage one of your client's awesome reviews into many positive links from multiple review websites. You'll learn how to get these multiple online reviews from your happiest customers using my simple, legitimate and unconventional strategy.

How will you find the time to implement these strategies? I'll show you how to accomplish this in 30 minutes or less per week for a small business. Have a larger business or need to delegate these duties to someone else? By understanding these strategies, you'll be able to train an employee, outside contractor or a legitimate reputation management firm to handle these for you! Are you envious of those customer service awards received by your competitors or other businesses? I'll show you how to go after those awards as well!

HOW TO GET THE MOST VALUE OUT OF THIS BOOK

Because I intend to quickly give you big value for your time and money, my books and courses give you top actionable tips that you can implement right now. My books and courses are no fluff, my stories are short . . . no rambling!

Take notes and write down your actionable goals! Don't just read the book and not take action. Most chapters end with specific action steps to take. Do them! If you don't have the time or need help, then delegate these tasks to a staff member or outside contractor. You don't have to implement these strategies verbatim! Even if you only implement half of them, they will have a profound impact on your business. Start with just one strategy! As you see your results improve from that one strategy, you'll want to do more.

Because resources are constantly being updated for these strategies, I created one page on my website that you can always access for the most up-to-date links. Check my website often (tomkenemore.com/fire) for updates and you can join my email list there as well.

For even more help with these strategies, join the companion online course and my best selling course! You and your friends can enroll for a special low rate (tomkenemore.com/reviewscourse)

Read the entire book now or as soon as possible. The longer you let this book sit on the virtual shelf, the bigger the chance you'll never read it or act on the strategies! So let's get started!

Chapter 2

Why Are You in Business?

If you are not willing to ask for feedback from your customers, then you shouldn't be in business!

— Tom Kenemore

ASSUMPTIONS AND A WARNING!

First off, I am assuming that you are offering a great product or service and are delivering it with exceptional customer service. **WARNING!** Do not use these strategies if you are selling a shoddy product or service. If your product or service is not great, fix it before implementing these strategies! Or ask yourself why you are in a business that is not offering a great product or service. Maybe a change in your business, product or service makes more sense to start with? I'll cover this even more later in the book, but I want to touch on it here right from the start. All of the awards I've mentioned in my DJ company were won because of offering a great service first! My talented staff and team of DJs worked very hard to please our clients and go above and beyond. So again, begin with a great product, service and fantastic customer service!

Before online reviews became popular, businesses with poor products or customer service could still survive because of a constant stream of unaware customers. That strategy is almost impossible to do now, which is a good thing. Despite all of the negativity from business owners about online reviews, they do make or encourage business owners to improve their products, services and customer service. After all, are you not in business to improve people's lives?

THE VALUE OF A HAPPY CUSTOMER!

Start thinking of your happy clients and customers as one of your most valuable assets. Your happy customers want to help you succeed and many will respond to your easy requests to help out in spreading the good word about your business. As social media expert Brian Solis said, "Welcome to a new era of marketing and service in which your brand is defined by those who experience it."

A stellar review from a client on a review website will do some, if not all of these:

- Give you a higher listing on the review website

- Increase your star rating on the site and in search engines that share it

- Increase organic national searches on Google, Yahoo, and more

- Increase your local search engine optimization, for example on Google Maps

- But most importantly, it will increase your social proof, your legitimacy in your market. Clients and customers buy from businesses and business owners that they trust. Legitimate online reviews will do that for you!

In this chapter I warned you about using these strategies if you are not offering a quality product or service. I also touched on the value of a happy customer. In the next chapter we will introduce you to some of the more popular review websites and tell you how to find the specific review websites for your industry.

Chapter 3

Introduction to Online Review Websites!

"If you are in a competitive industry, great online reviews are not just nice to have, they are a requirement!"

— Tom Kenemore

WHAT ARE ONLINE REVIEW WEBSITES?

An online review website may be a search engine, a social media website, a free or paid directory, or a combination of all of these. Nowadays it's hard to tell the difference! Many review websites now act more like social media sites with friending, liking, commenting and such. Some social media websites like Facebook have a review component to their local business pages.

Some online review websites are a grouping of businesses by industry and may be free or require payment. Some review websites are paid advertising sites. For the most part, I won't be differentiating between them. Most paid review websites still publish your profile and allow posting of your reviews for free. Just because a review website offers paid advertising doesn't mean you have to buy it. For example, Yelp, Google and Facebook all offer paid advertising, but their free, organic search results are still huge.

WHAT REVIEW WEBSITES SHOULD YOU TARGET?

So what review websites should you target? Well that depends on your industry, but listed below are some of the top ones for most types of businesses. Please note that some of these sites are social media properties or directories. Even though they may not have a direct review component, you can still use reviews received from your clients in the descriptions and/or in posts on most of these websites.

Because of continual updates to the list of review websites, you can find my full list with links at my companion blog post (tomkenemore.com/reviewsites). At that post you'll find specific review websites for industries including healthcare, food, travel, employers and more. If you have other online review websites or directories to recommend, please add them to the comments at that blog post.

MAJOR ONLINE REVIEW WEBSITES AND SOCIAL MEDIA:

- Google My Business: www.google.com/business
- Bing Places for business: www.bingplaces.com
- Yelp: biz.yelp.com
- Yahoo Local: smallbusiness.yahoo.com/local-listings
- Facebook page: www.facebook.com/pages/create.php
- Foursquare: business.foursquare.com/claim
- Twitter: twitter.com
- Angie's List: business.angieslist.com/Registration/SimpleRegistration.aspx
- Citysearch: www.citysearch.com
- LinkedIn Business page: www.linkedin.com/company/add/show

Find Your Industry-Specific Review Websites

Now, let's find some industry-specific review websites for your business. Open up a new tab in your Internet browser and pull up Google Search. Type in your general industry name followed by the word "reviews." You may want to do this search on several of your industry keywords. Check each organic link in your search on the first few pages. Review and directory websites that pop up on page one or two of Google may be websites you should join.

Time for some hands on training! You can follow along with me in this video (tomkenemore.com/reviewvideo). While you are there, be sure to subscribe to my Youtube Channel to receive all of my video tips!

For example, let's say your industry is wedding DJs, like mine used to be. You would type in "wedding DJ reviews" in Google. Depending on where you are in the world when you do it, there will be different results. In general, you would first see the sponsored ads on the top of the page which we will ignore since we are not talking about Google Adwords. Then you should see the Google Local pages with reviews followed by the organic searches. Of the suggested review websites, Yelp will probably show up. Typically two or more wedding specific review websites show up as well, like WeddingWire and TheKnot. This is not a surprise as these are both websites that I had profiles on when I owned my wedding DJ company. You'll have to investigate your industry-specific review websites to see which ones make sense to join.

This is a search that you will want to do a couple times a year at a minimum. There will always be new review websites joining the Internet and some that may change or discontinue service. You may also hear of others worth signing up for as you network within your specific industry. Again, you can find many industry specific websites on my blog post mentioned earlier.

Claim or Set Up Your First Online Review Profile – Google My Business!

Now, let's claim your first review website profile! My recommendation would be to claim or set up your Google My Business profile first. As of this writing, only Google Local business pages can accept reviews. However, you could certainly post your awesome online reviews on your brand page if that is the type of Google page you set up. Maybe in the future, Google will allow your customers to post reviews to your brand page or someone will create an app for that feature.

As you may have noticed, Google My Business pages show up really high in local search results. So much could be said about the command presence that Google has on the Internet. Google has been making many large and small changes to how their business listings work and how they work with Google Maps. One thing stays consistent; Google has a strong emphasis on reviews! So start with your Google My Business profile first!

Here is another video (tomkenemore.com/googlevideo) showing the initial set up and claiming of your Google My Business profile. Keep in mind this process may change as Google continues to make updates. Once you get five reviews posted on your Google My Business local page, your star rating will start being shown. This is a nice little bonus Google gives you so you stand out of the crowd of businesses that have zero to four reviews.

Do you have multiple locations or branches for your business? If so, you will need to set up separate profiles for each location on most of the review websites. I know that sounds like a pain, but it's actually a good thing. You'll be able to track and compare how each location is doing, set up competitions for which location can get the highest ratings and more!

Google Seller Ratings

Larger companies and brands will benefit from Google Seller Ratings (GSR). Your GSR acts similar to your local profile when you get more than five reviews with a key difference. Your Google Seller Ratings appear in your Google Adwords ad text. Generally you need at least thirty reviews within a twelve-month period and an overall rating of 3.5 or better. Google admits to allowing some businesses this distinction with even fewer reviews. This is a really nice feature if you use Google Adwords. Plus Google provides this for no additional charge. For more on Google Seller Ratings, check out our resource webpage (tomkenemore.com/fire).

WHAT PROFILE TO SET UP NEXT? YELP!

Yelp shows up very high in Google Search, so you want as many Yelp reviews that you can get. For example, in my wedding DJ business, our Yelp listing made it to the bottom of page one in Google Search and that was only with a few reviews showing up! Before we started with Yelp, Yelp didn't even show up in the wedding DJ category or was buried pages deep in Google. Plus, as of this writing, Yelp reviews are syndicated to Yahoo.com, another popular search engine. Other review websites may do this as well further leveraging your efforts on Yelp. I'll cover more about Yelp later on.

SOCIAL MEDIA PROFILES WITH POTENTIAL FOR ONLINE REVIEW COMPONENTS

Facebook: You probably already have a Facebook page for your business. If not, I would recommend setting one up if appropriate for your industry. Make sure your business page is listed as a local business or a category that allows online reviews. I made this mistake when changing our Facebook page from being a local business page. All of our nice reviews disappeared and were never recovered! So learn from my mistake!

Administrators currently have the ability to respond to reviews posted on your Facebook review tab. You also have the ability to remove the review or rating system as well. Check out our resource webpage for more about adding ratings and reviews to your Facebook business page.

Twitter: If you don't have a Twitter account for your business, I would recommend setting one of those up. You can post excerpts from reviews that you have received and also ask your customers to tweet a review as well. Start a hashtag like #yourbusinessnamereviews so you can collect as many positive reviews that are easily searchable. Favorite those tweets as well. Research shows that positive tweets from customers can lead to more business. For more on setting up a Twitter profile for your business see our resource webpage.

MORE ABOUT SETTING UP ONLINE REVIEW PROFILES

Each review website profile set up is going to be different. So I'm not going to go into detail on how to set up each one. Plus, with all of the changes and updates going on, within a few months, my recommendations could be out of date. You will find that most profile forms are intuitive and easy to set up quickly.

I'm also not advocating that you become an expert on each of these review websites. Who has the time for that? Just fill out each profile as completely as possible. Be sure to use some keywords in the business description, but don't over "stuff it" with keywords for your industry. You can always come back and add more information later. Once you get a few profiles completed, you'll start sending them happy clients ready to write reviews, which I'll cover in the next chapter.

Consider starting with just a few review website profiles and then add more if your volume of reviews warrants it. Trying to stay on top of more than 10 review websites is a lot of work and if it spreads your reviews really thin, it may not give your business the impact you were looking for.

TO CLAIM OR NOT TO CLAIM YOUR EXISTING BUSINESS PROFILES

If your profile has already been automatically posted by the review website, you may not have a choice but to claim it and start filling it out. First, check what your existing profile and online reviews look like. If you don't have any, or if they are all positive, then go ahead and claim it. If you have poor reviews or your rating is less than you would like, check to see if you can establish a new profile. We did this for two of our paid wedding DJ advertising website review profiles. Since I had been in business for over twenty years, customers on their own had been posting online reviews so there was a mix of positive and negative ones. So instead of trying to boost a lower score, we just started new profiles. Our new profiles quickly became more noticed than the older ones because those were the only profiles we sent new happy clients to in order to fill out reviews.

A quick word of caution. It is reported that Google can move reviews from one profile to another, so it is possible if you try to escape your bad reviews from an old profile, they may come back to haunt you! This also happened to one of our paid wedding profiles after I had sold the business. The review website took an old profile and combined it with the new profile, increasing the overall amount of reviews and maybe the SEO, but dropping the star rating!

TAKE ACTION

Now for your first take action exercise! I want you to claim or create at least one new review profile for your business. I would recommend either your Google My Business profile, Yelp or Facebook page, or choose one from my list (tomkenemore.com/reviewsites). Then fill it out with your business information. If you haven't opened your business up yet for customers, you can still set up profiles and start engaging future customers with your content.

CONCLUSION TO ONLINE REVIEW WEBSITES

In this chapter I covered what a review website is and named some of the top review websites. I explained how you can find the specific review websites for your industry and I gave you some tips on filling out a profile. Plus I covered whether to claim or not to claim an existing review website profile. Make sure you complete this chapter's action steps. Get all of my bonus content for this chapter and the book right here (tomkenemore.com/firebonuses). Now, in the next chapter we will start collecting those awesome reviews from your customers!

Chapter 4

Introduction to Getting Great Reviews

"Feedback is the breakfast of champions!"

– Ken Blanchard

INTRODUCTION

In this chapter you will learn how to start getting reviews from your clients and customers. I'll show you a simple letter and email template that you can use and modify for your specific company's needs. Now let's start getting those Fans on Fire reviews!

HOW WILL YOU GET YOUR CUSTOMER'S REVIEWS?

You can use several methods to get client reviews. You could also use just one method, but I recommend using as many as you have time for! Why employ multiple ways to get reviews? Great reviews are like gold and often-times a customer will ignore the first or second request to write a review. Think about it; how many times have you been contacted to complete a survey, write a review, etc. Your customers and clients are inundated with these requests. If you ask your clients multiple times using different methods, you will likely get more reviews. Not every customer is going to reply, but you don't need them to. You only need a small percentage of customers to reply to make this worthwhile. In my wedding DJ company, on average, we received about 40% of our review forms back completed, which is a high percentage. Your business could receive more or less.

Stop! Important!

DO NOT send clients directly to your review website profiles at this point! Why? Simply because we don't know what they are going to say about you or your company. All initial reviews will come directly to you so you have a chance to sort them out. And that part will be covered in the next chapter. There are three possible exceptions to this rule:

1. If you own a very small single operator company and you personally work with every customer or client. You know with almost a 100% certainty that your customer is happy with you.

2. The second exception would be that you are so confident in your business, product or service that you think everyone is going to give you a great review. Or you simply don't mind the occasional lower review and feel that this is a simpler way to run your Fans on Fire system. I would caution against this, but I know some of you will anyway.

3. The third exception to that rule would be a "Fans on Fire" in the moment. That's when you are face to face or on the phone and your customer is raving about how great your business is. Don't miss out on the opportunity to get an awesome online review right then and there. Start by asking your happy customer to post on one review website; then keep going, and you might get them to complete several different review websites while you are talking to them! Just keep asking until your customer sounds bored or has to leave. Make a note on your phone, computer, or cash register to remember this. Tell your employees to watch for "Fans on Fire" in the moment opportunities.

A couple words of warning. If your customer is at your place of business, it's best if they use their own smart phone on their own data plan. For sure do not set up a tablet, computer or laptop to use for reviews. Google and other websites may monitor your IP address and more to find any reviews that appear suspicious. Suspicious reviews may get blocked from being shown. Or worse!

POPULAR WAYS TO COLLECT ONLINE REVIEWS

Here are some methods for getting client reviews:

- Link to a survey or review form from your email or your cash register receipt
- Comment card on your restaurant table
- Comment card on your store's register
- Email a link or comment review form to a customer after a sale. Reminders could still be sent months after the sale to see how your product is working for them
- Mail the review or survey form to your customer

IS THERE AN APP FOR THAT?

Your customer relationship management (CRM) software may already have a built in review system as well or maybe it can be customized or programmed. Your email program can also have an autoresponder set up to send requests for feedback automatically. There are also a number of custom application programs that you can use. Because of all the updates to this area, see my companion blog post (tomkenemore.com/reviewapps) for the latest information on software and apps that are available. Feel free to add your program or service in the comments if it is not listed.

Using an application or software program will certainly save time. This book can serve as your guide to make sure it is set up correctly and getting you the results you want. If you have a small amount of customers or you prefer something simple, I've included an Excel file spreadsheet template for tracking your reviews on the book resources webpage (tomkenemore.com/fire).

What Questions to Ask Your Customers

You need to choose what customer information you will ask for. Certain industries may have data privacy requirements, so keep that in mind. Here are some sample questions I recommend including on your review request form:

- Date of sale/service performed
- Full name
- Mailing address
- Email address
- Phone number
- How happy are you with our company/product or service?
  - » 5 – very happy
  - » 4 – happy
  - » 3 – just average
  - » 2 – unhappy
  - » 1 – very unhappy
- If not a 5, please tell us what would make it a "5" experience for you?
- Please write a review of our services so that we may share it with others like you:

Make sure to ask for the initial review as close as possible to the purchase time or completion of service date. If you wait weeks or months to ask for a review, there is a higher chance that the customer won't respond. With that being said, you can certainly send them a reminder of how important their feedback is weeks and even months afterward if they never responded to your first request. Did you get behind or have you never asked for reviews before? Depending on your product or service, you can sometimes go back multiple years and ask for reviews. Remember that a happy client or raving fan customer is like marketing gold; don't let them slip through the cracks! I have received reviews from clients almost a full year after we provided our wedding DJ service!

SAMPLE INITIAL REVIEW REQUEST FORM

So here is the wording from a sample initial review request form, letter or email. Options or my notes will appear in brackets. Be sure to delete my notes before sending to your clients:

Dear (Client/customer first name)

Thank you for (purchasing x product on date/choosing our x service on date, etc.) from my company. I certainly hope you are enjoying your purchase (service, etc.). My team and I really appreciate your business.

Could you help me out? Feedback from our customers is important to us! If you could take a few moments to fill out the questions below, I would appreciate it. I have enclosed a postage paid envelope for your convenience (If mailing a letter, including a postage paid envelope will increase your response rate).

(OPTIONAL TEXT:)

(You could also add: "Also, your written comments directly affect my staff's bonus pay. So please be sure to return this right away." Do you offer an incentive to your staff for helping to generate great reviews? I recommend you do!)

(ALSO, WE LOVE TO GET PICTURES AND/OR VIDEO OF OUR CLIENTS ENJOYING OUR PRODUCT/SERVICE IF POSSIBLE.)

PLEASE CIRCLE OR COMPLETE BELOW (INSERT YOUR QUESTIONS HERE or link to your online form; remember, don't ask for any information you really don't need; the fewer the questions the better):

Date of sale/service performed?

Your phone #

Your full name

Email address

Mailing address

How happy are you with our (company/product or service)?

5 – very happy 4 – happy 3 – just average 2 – unhappy 1 – very unhappy

If not a 5, please tell us what would make it a "5" experience for you? (This is where you will get suggestions on improving your product or service.)

Please write a review of our services so that we may share it with others like you (please use back of page if needed.):

(Allow space for the written review; this is very important; give them plenty of room to write a long, awesome review about you!)

Remember, (your company name) offers (your other kinds of products/services). We depend on referrals for most of our business. ***THANK YOU IN ADVANCE FOR YOUR REFERRALS; WE REALLY APPRECIATE IT!***

Please let us know how we can be of service to you in the future. Thank you for helping make (your company name) the best it can be!

Sincerely,

Your name & direct contact info (No review profiles or social media links yet!)

You can download this initial review letter/email form here (tomkenemore.com/firebonuses) as well as all of our bonus templates. Just edit the template for your product or service or use for ideas on creating your own form letter. Keep this in mind though. The longer the form, the longer it takes a client to fill it out and you will receive fewer completed comment forms. Make sure every question is relevant and important to you. Feel free to experiment, though. Your market may respond better to different questions, different contact methods and/or different contact frequencies.

MAKE IT EASY . . . MAKE IT SHORT!

Let me get on my soapbox for a minute. Make every question on your initial review form fight for its life! In today's society, we are "formed" to death! Everywhere we go, a business or an organization has some questionnaire or survey they want us to fill out. Help reduce the form madness by keeping your initial review form as short and as easy to complete as possible. Ok, rant over! Now, with that being said, other possible questions you may want to use are:

- How did you find out about our product/service/company?
- What made you choose our product/service/company over a competitor? (This is the question that I used to find out that our online reviews were the most important deciding factor for choosing us over the competition!)
- How easy was it to do business with us?
- Would you recommend us to a friend?

BE OPEN TO THE DELIVERY METHOD!

Don't get stuck on requiring that reviews come back only on one of your forms. You may get phone calls, emails, texts, Facebook messages, etc. All of those are super valuable and can be used in the next step, leveraging your great initial reviews. You can also use your customer's comments and reviews to get valuable information about how you and your team are doing or how to make improvements to your product or service. Remember, feedback is the breakfast of champions!

To INCENTIVIZE OR NOT?

Should you offer an incentive to your customer to fill out this initial review? I recommend that you ***DO NOT*** offer an incentive to get a review! Case in point: Years ago in my wedding DJ business, we held a drawing from customers that returned the initial review form. The drawing would be for a low cost gift certificate to a restaurant or local business. My theory was that it would help encourage more customers to complete the review form. However, I believe this was perceived as a gimmick by our clients. Plus, when I looked at the results, we got back more reviews when we didn't offer an incentive. By not offering an incentive in our communication with clients, we were able to more clearly focus on how important their review was to us. Also, when it comes to asking your happy clients to post reviews on your online profiles, most of the review websites have specific rules or guidelines against "bribing" or rewarding your customers for reviews.

Do You HAVE A BRAND NEW BUSINESS?

Are you just starting your business and have zero customers? How do you get reviews then? If you have already sold some of your product in a test market or have worked your business as a hobby, you can ask those customers for a review. If not, do a great job with your first few customers and ask for the review! Consider selling some of your product or service as a test marketing strategy. You can sell your product at a discount during a soft launch or pre-opening and collect some great reviews to use for your official marketing launch. If it is financially feasible, give away some of your product or service and ask for feedback. You may choose to send your product to a blogger or podcaster in hopes that they will mention or review your product online.

I don't recommend this strategy, but some businesses do ask their friends and family to write reviews. Unless they are legitimate customers, don't ask your friends or family members to write you a review. I have several reasons for this. First, as a business owner, you want to be proud of each and every review that you and your team worked hard to get. So when you get to a milestone of say 25 – 5 star reviews, you know they are all 100% earned. Secondly, and maybe more importantly, many of the review websites are finding new and unique ways to search for reviews that could be fake. So again, work the Fans on Fire system legitimately and your reviews will come!

NEVER, NEVER, EVER BUY REVIEWS!

You may have gotten these emails or messages already. The email subject line reads something like this: "I'll write you xx reviews for your product or service for $xx". Just hit delete on these offers and move on. Or maybe you are looking for some low cost freelance help on the Fiverr website and you run across an ad to write you a review for $5. Do not get tempted by these kinds of shortcuts to a great online reputation. You will likely get caught and penalized by that search engine or review website. Build a business with a strong reputation and with strong integrity. If you were to win an award or otherwise become famous in your industry because of a load of purchased reviews, you will get caught, and the results could be very costly to your company and personal reputation. The media and public do not think kindly toward businesses that cheat the system. Just turn on the TV news. Every week it seems like there is another business getting caught for cheating at something. So don't do it! It's challenging enough to run a legitimate, ethical and honest business!

MULTIPLE ONLINE REVIEWS FROM A SINGLE SALE

You can sometimes get more than one review from a single sale. Maybe the customer's spouse, significant other, friends or an associate that also experienced your product or service will write a great review for you as well? Many review websites do not verify that reviewers actually purchased the product. This is perfectly legitimate on many of the review website platforms.

For example, think of a happy table of patrons at your restaurant. If there are six people having a great time in your establishment, why not get a review from all of them and not just the one picking up the tab. This is a great Fans on Fire in the moment opportunity as I previously mentioned. You could get multiple positive online reviews from this one happy group of patrons. Just have a special card printed up with one or two of your review profiles on it with short links so they can access them quickly from their smart phones.

CONCLUSION AND ACTIONS!

In this chapter we talked about many ways of getting the initial review from your clients. I also gave you some sample questions to ask during the initial review process. Plus we covered a strategy to get reviews if you haven't officially opened your business yet. Now for your next actions! Before you go to the next chapter, create an initial review form for your business. It can be online, an email or a letter you will mail. Now, send it out to at least 10 past customers, if you have that many. Get all of my bonus content for this chapter and the book right here (tomkenemore.com/firebonuses). For even more help with these strategies, join the companion online course and my best selling course (tomkenemore.com/reviewscourse). Then, in the next chapter, I'll tell you how to leverage the great reviews you get back and how to turn them into marketing gold for your business!

Chapter 5

Fans on Fire – Leverage Your Great Client Reviews

"Business is war and positive online reviews are your elite Special Forces soldiers!"

– Tom Kenemore

INTRODUCTION

Now for the fun part! This is where the Fans on Fire system gets very powerful! I am going to show you how to leverage those awesome initial reviews you just received from your customers or clients. You are going to send *__ONLY__* your clients that wrote amazing initial reviews to your online review profiles. That's right! You will select the customers that you want to write on your online review profiles.

You might be thinking that this is a form of manipulation because we are only encouraging positive reviewers to go to these external review websites. Well this strategy is just formalizing what you would likely be doing anyway. For example, if a client came to you with a complaint, you wouldn't tell them to review you on Yelp would you? Of course not! That would be shooting yourself in the foot. You would handle the complaint directly with your customer. Or another way to think about it is if you were putting together a list of printed testimonials to send to potential clients. Like in the old days! You wouldn't include a negative review on that printed list would you? Would you include a negative review on your own website? Probably not!

To go even further. Google, Yelp, Facebook, etc. are all businesses too. They are not non-profit organizations set up to protect consumers like the Better Business Bureau. You can bet that the rules these businesses play by are to make a profit. We are just utilizing their rules and websites to benefit your business. Hey, business is war and positive online reviews are your elite Special Forces soldiers! What soldiers would you send out to battle for you? Your awesome review soldiers will help you battle any fake or negative reviews you may receive.

Even after all of that explanation, you can still choose to bypass this step and send every customer to your online review profiles. Some would argue that the more online reviews you receive, regardless of quality, the better. The reality is you get to choose the strategies that fit you and your business goals.

Start with Just One Review

When you are just starting out, you may not have a lot of initial reviews to handle. No worries; you can start with just one client's initial review. If you have just a few customer reviews to work with, I recommend processing them as they come in. Once you are receiving more than five per week, I would suggest batching them once per day or once per week.

Organize Those Reviews

Now you need to sort those initial reviews. Start by removing any duplicate reviews. If your customer management software allows it, mark that transaction or customer as *feedback received*. Be sure to include initial reviews received via other methods as well (by phone, text, email, message, etc.). Have someone type up the review if it is on a card or on a paper form, or you can do it yourself. I'm a slow typist so I paid my daughter to type them for my wedding DJ company. Then I recommend printing your reviews so you can keep them organized in one place.

Ideally you would be able to add the comments to the customer's record in your management software and categorize them in at least three ways:

- Fans on Fire – 4.5 to 5 stars! This is a great or an amazing initial review; you will be moving them to the next step.

- Average Fan – This is your 3 to 4 star ratings. Kind of average to slightly above average review, but not enough to move on to the next level. The program stops for this client. The only exception would be if your marketing goal is to have as many reviews as possible on a particular review website. Depending on the review website, having more reviews increases your ranking, SEO, etc., so that may be more important than having a near perfect overall rating.

- Not a Fan. Oh no, a 1 or 2 star rating! Definitely not moving on to the next Fans on Fire step, but I'll give you some strategies for how to handle complaints in the last chapter.

If your customer management software won't allow the labeling, tagging or notes mentioned in the last section, you can also use a simple spreadsheet in Excel or Google docs to track your reviews. You can get my sample Excel file template from the book resources webpage. For now, decide on a cut-off point to get into your Fans on Fire system, or use my example from the last section. This is an important decision! The cut-off point in client satisfaction will directly affect the number of ratings and the level of ratings you receive online.

CONTACT YOUR FANS ON FIRE!

Now that you are organized, decide how you are going to contact your Fans on Fire. In the bonus downloads (tomkenemore.com/firebonuses), I've included several example emails or letters you can use and customize. Get your free download templates now if you haven't already. Customize the text or if the words don't fit you, write your own. These are **_YOUR_** customers; be authentic in your request and they will respond. Believe me! Happy customers want to help businesses they love! Your request of them is an easy and simple way for them to reciprocate for your great product and customer service!

SAMPLE FIRST FANS ON FIRE EMAIL OR LETTER

Sample text, First Fans on Fire email or letter with optional comments. Be sure to delete my notes before sending to your clients:

Dear (client first name)

Thank you again for your business and thank you so much for your positive comments. It is the highlight of my day to see a great review from a satisfied client/customer!

Can I ask a really important favor of you? Could you please take a few moments to review your purchase on the websites below? Your great review of our company is so important in sharing our products with future customers!

(Optional: To make it easier, any written comments you made are below and you can cut and paste them to re-use them on the first website; then please write a different review or change the wording on the additional websites. (This helps avoid any duplicate review/content issues.))

(Cut and paste the clients review comments here)

(If no comments or you are in a hurry, you can give us a rating only on most of the websites.)

Yelp (hyperlink text or type out link to your Yelp profile)

Facebook page – "Like" our page and click the review tab (hyperlink text or type out link to your Facebook page if you have reviews activated)

Google (hyperlink text or type out link to your My Business profile)

& if you would please: (link to your Fans on Fire page on your website) (for several other websites)

Thank you so much for your help! Reviews and referrals are more important to us than ever before. From all of us at (your company name), thank you again for your business, reviews, referrals, and most of all, your passion and enthusiasm for what we do!

Sincerely

Your name

Contact information

Your website, social media, etc. (Yes, finally!! You can use these!)

DO NOT MASS EMAIL!

I don't recommend mass emailing to your Fans on Fire clients. Take time to email your customers individually so the messages get to your customers and are not filtered as spam. Send these as plain text emails with as few links as possible. Also, send them from a personalized email address, not a main company email. The strategy here is to engage your customer personally so they will want to post an online review for you. The only exception would be a mass email to your fans in order to win a specific award or remind them of an approaching deadline, which I'll cover in the next chapter.

CONTACT YOUR FANS REGULARLY

Collect your positive initial reviews for the week and set a time to process them. If you are not able to do them daily, I recommend batching them on Tuesdays. Doing this consistently helps with regularity and helps improve your ranking on some of the review websites. Now, just because you are doing it regularly, doesn't mean your clients will respond regularly. It may take your client anywhere from a few minutes to weeks to write the online review. In a recent BrightLocal Consumer Review Survey, 69% of consumer's say an online review needs to have a date within 2-3 months in order to be considered relevant.

How to Contact Your Fans

I recommend using all forms of communication with your clients. For example, if the first Fans on Fire client you process has a physical address, email and phone number in your customer database, use all of those methods. First, try calling them. You can use the sample text from the previous email/letter as the basis for a script, but again, be authentic, never pushy or desperate. In your conversation or voice mail, thank them for the nice review. Tell them how the review made you feel, how pumped you were to tell your staff about it. Ask them for an additional favor, could they please write another review on Yelp, Google, or whatever review website(s) you are targeting. Tell them how important it is for you, your employees and your business.

If you are leaving a voice mail, tell them to look for an email or letter from you for the links to the review website(s). If you are talking to your customer live on the phone, email them the first letter with links as you are talking. If you catch a customer at the right time, you may be able to get multiple online reviews from them while you are on the phone chatting. Just keep the conversation going and send more links as they review you. Now if you leave a message, go ahead and email and mail the first Fans on Fire letter. If you are not comfortable calling your client and asking for this, just use the other contact methods. But remember, using all forms of contact information will maximize your results. At a minimum, use the contact method that the initial review came through: phone call, email, text, Facebook message, etc.

How Often Should You Contact Your Fans?

The big question! How often should you pester your clients for a review? I recommend a total of 4 to 6 contact dates to your client when working the entire Fans on Fire process. Please keep in mind that a contact date may include multiple types of contact methods, like an email, phone call, mail, etc. If you contact your client more than that, you risk being annoying, and possibly turning a happy client into an upset client.

Even with my recommended amount of contacting, you could still receive complaints. Why do I recommend this then? Well this goes back to one of my rules for sales. If you are not getting 1 or 2 out of a 100 contacts complaining about your level of contacting, you are not contacting enough! If you don't contact your happy fans enough, you are missing out! We are all simply inundated with distractions these days. Your request for a review has to cut through the mountain of email, mail and messages we all receive each day. Just make sure your client contacts are spaced out and strategic!

Studies show the best timing for mailing, emailing or calling a client depends upon the type of business you are in. My suggestion would be to schedule these contacts at different times and days of the week. For example, schedule the first contact on a Tuesday morning, second contact on a Thursday evening, and a third contact on a weekend, etc. That way you improve your chances of reaching your client and requesting a quick review. Here is a sample schedule; but feel free to make adjustments to reflect your preference and comfort level:

- Email and/or mail initial review form at the time of purchase or within 48 hours.
  - » If no review is received after seven days, follow up with another email and/or mailing to get that initial review.
  - » If no review is received after fourteen more days, follow up a final time for the initial review with mail and/or email. Plus, consider a personal phone call/message to the client asking them to fill out the initial review.
- Make first Fans on Fire review contact as soon as you receive the positive review, or as soon as possible, or weekly on Tuesdays. Use mail, email and a phone call.
- Make second Fans on Fire review contact three to four weeks later by mail or email.
- Make third and final Fans on Fire review contact by mail, email and phone call one to two months later or before the end of an award period (see the Portable Document File (PDF) letters on the bonus download webpage if you are working to receive a specific reward; many end their qualifications on specific dates or at the end of the year).

Be sure to use the second or third sample contact emails and letters with both fans that have already reviewed you online and those that have not yet done so. Those templates are included in the bonus downloads (tomkenemore.com/firebonuses). As you will notice, those letters are worded to include all of your fans. Some alternate letters are there for use if you choose to target fans that have already reviewed you on at least one online review profile.

MAKE THE TIME!

I know you are busy and probably think you have very little time to spend on this, but resolve to spend at least thirty minutes per week on your Fans on Fire project and it will pay off for your business! If you don't have the time, have an assistant do it, an employee, an outside contractor, or anyone you trust to do detailed work. Don't miss out on the best marketing money can't buy!

UNIQUE REVIEWS JUST A FEW AT A TIME!

As you may have noticed from the sample letters, you want to ask your customer to re-write your positive review on two to three review websites maximum (at least on the first contact letter or email). I used to ask happy clients to review us on ten or more websites in my first email or letter, but we received a much lower response rate. Now, after the main two or three targeted review websites, just include a link to your Fans on Fire webpage that lists all of them. (I'll tell you how to set that up that webpage in the next chapter.) So if the client is a raving fan about your business, they have the option to review you on all of your profiles. And yes, some clients will do all of them.

Plus, it's important that each online review be unique for that client or significantly different from the others. I used to ask clients just to cut and paste the same text review across multiple review websites, but that can cause problems. You could get your duplicate reviews removed, or worse, get banned from a particular review website. Yelp and Google now aggressively search for duplicate and fake reviews. For example, my wedding DJ company served a large area in Minnesota. So to help with local search, I set up multiple Google Business Pages in four of the larger cities that we served. We were successful in getting several raving fans to cut and paste their identical reviews across all of our Google Pages. However, at some point Google removed the duplicate reviews, not just on three of the

Google Pages, but all four! So now those awesome client reviews only exist on other non-Google review websites. So learn from my mistake!

HOW DO YOU GET NOTIFIED OF AN ONLINE REVIEW?

So how do you know when you receive a new review on one of your online profiles? Some review websites will email or text you when you receive a new online review, but some will not. I made it a habit to check those websites manually about once per week or at a minimum, bi-weekly. Also, check the notification settings on each online review profile to make sure the notifications are set up the way you want. If you are using a software or app to track online mentions of your company, then it should be set to automatically notify you of receiving an online review. Setting up a free Google Alert for your company name is still another option. However, I've had mixed results from Google Alerts and still prefer to manually check for new online reviews. For more on setting up a Google Alert and other methods for monitoring your reviews, check out the book resources webpage (tomkenemore.com/fire).

CONGRATULATIONS! YOU RECEIVED AN AWESOME ONLINE REVIEW!

Hooray! You received a great review on an online review website! First, do your happy dance! Whooo Hoooo! Great job! You just added a tremendous marketing asset to your company! So now what? If the review website allows you to comment on the review, be sure to do so. Thank the customer again publicly for their business and kind words. Be humble and appreciative! If there are social media type functions available, like or love the review as well. If you can "follow" or "friend" the reviewer, that may provide some further marketing benefits. By taking these actions, you become an engaged business owner that cares about what their customers think and feel about your business. Plus your comments on the review add to the content of your review profile, potentially helping with your search engine optimization on that profile.

MONITOR THE MIX

Keep track of the number of reviews and the dates they are posted to your online profiles. In general, you want to get reviews spread somewhat evenly along your highest priority review website profiles. You can accomplish this by alternating the websites that you target in your contacts to your happy clients. For example, if your Google profile has received a lot of reviews lately, maybe target Yelp or Facebook with your current client contacts. If a review website has not received a fresh review in a month or so, be sure to target that one. You can easily change the order of the review website links in your emails and letters to accomplish this. Or replace or remove a website profile temporarily on your contact letters and emails if needed.

Remember my list of review websites (tomkenemore.com/reviewsites). Depending on your industry, a great review on Google may be far more valuable than a review on another website. That doesn't mean you ignore these other websites entirely. For example, your target goal mix could be that for every ten online reviews you get, you might want four of them on Google, three of them on Yelp, and the remaining reviews on other websites. Can you really control this mix? Yes, again, by changing the review websites that you target in your client contacts. I estimate that you can have about an 80% control of your review profile mix. Let me know what your results are (tk@tomkenemore.com).

Remember that according to a survey, the majority of consumers said an online review needed to be less than three months old in order to be considered relevant. So spread the online review requests around, but make it your goal to get at least one online review posted per quarter per review website profile. If you have a lot of customers, then make it your goal to get one review per month (or per week) per profile or add more review profiles. Remember to feed the content hungry animal Google! The more current reviews you have on a review profile, the more likely that profile will rank high in Google and maybe make it onto page one! Plus listings and reviews on a diversity of websites can also help with your local search engine optimization and rank your main website higher.

For example, my wedding DJ company had four page one listings on Google at the same time! We had our Google My Business profile, our main website, our business Facebook page and our Yelp profile all on page one of Google for several important keyword searches. Since Google currently shows only ten organic listings per page, having four of those ten listings increased our chances of getting traffic. Plus it pushed some of our competition to page two on those Google searches!

CONCLUSION TO LEVERAGING GREAT REVIEWS AND ACTIONS

In this chapter you learned the core strategies of the Fans on Fire review leveraging system! You learned about organizing your reviews and contacting your fans to get online reviews. Your next action for this chapter is to create your first Fans on Fire email or letter and send it to your qualified fans. Remember, if you have a lot of qualified fans already, spread them around different review websites. Just don't bombard a single review website with too many fans at one time. Get all of my bonus content for this chapter and the book (tomkenemore.com/firebonuses). I really want to hear about the results you get from your initial review contacts! So be sure to email me (tk@tomkenemore.com). In the next chapter you'll find out how to set up your Fans on Fire webpage, how to go after a specific business award and so much more!

Chapter 6

Fans on Fire II – More Strategies to Leverage Your Great Client Reviews

"A new currency is emerging online; your likes, comments (positive and negative), follows, and shares are sometimes worth more than money!"

– Tom Kenemore

INTRODUCTION

There are so many more ways to leverage your client's great reviews! In this chapter I'll show you how to set up your Fans on Fire webpage. Does your business deserve an award? I'll show you how to use your awesome client reviews to go after those customer service awards as well. How can you use reviews to incentivize and evaluate employees? I'll tell you how and so much more!

YOUR FANS ON FIRE WEBPAGE

A Fans on Fire webpage is a secret, hidden page on your website that you will set up just for your fans. The Fans on Fire webpage contains all of the links of review websites that you would like a happy client to complete for you. This is your ultimate goal when sending out your Fans on Fire letters and emails. In my experience, you'll want to put the link to your Fans on Fire webpage in the third or fourth position in your letters and emails. Just how many of your fans will follow that link and complete all of these review websites? It's hard to say, but the more happy clients you have, the more that will want to do this for you!

When designing your Fans on Fire webpage, you can use text only or use logo or graphics for the links. This page should only be accessible to clients you give the link to. Again, I highly recommend **NOT** making this webpage public or a part of your website navigation or menus. Also, you may want to change the order of the links on your Fans on Fire webpage from time to time based on the websites that need more review attention. Insert the link to this webpage in the appropriate spot on your Fans on Fire letters and emails. Keep the link short in printed letters or use a URL reducer like bit.ly so it is easier for your fans to type out on a computer, tablet or smartphone. You could also set up a Quick Response code (QR code) for that webpage as well, if appropriate for your customers. You will find links for both URL reducers and free QR code generators on the book resources webpage (tomkenemore.com/fire).

Although I've never tried it, you could experiment by having a video introduction embedded on your Fans on Fire webpage. I can imagine an authentic video from you, the owner or manager of your business, thanking your client for the kind words. You can tell them how much it means to receive praise from a happy client like them and then ask for one more favor. To please click on the links below and share their thoughts with future clients. Another thought would be a short video on how to navigate each review website in order to leave a review. Even though a review website may seem easy for you to navigate, some of your more technically challenged clients may struggle with it. Remember, it's all about increasing the number of awesome reviews. I would bet that videos like these will increase your overall reviews. Ok, so how about a challenge? The first reader to test this video idea and email me a link (tk@tomkenemore.com) gets a free gift! Who will test this idea first?

If you service clients in different market segments or multiple locations, you may want to set up different Fans on Fire webpages to service each segment or location. For example in my DJ company, our main market focus was weddings. However, we also serviced private, school and business clients. So we set up two different Fans on Fire webpages to account for the difference. The only difference between the two webpages was the removal of the wedding-related review websites for the second group of clients. An alternative sample layout and text for your Fans on Fire webpage is available in the bonus downloadable templates.

Sample Text Fans on Fire Webpage

Here is the main sample text for your Fans on Fire webpage. Be sure to delete my notes before posting on your website:

Please take a few moments and rate and review our service on **ALL** of the websites below (**or at least down to and including Citysearch**). *Please use a unique and new review on each website.* It really does go quickly... THANK YOU SO MUCH!

No comments or in a hurry? Please give us a rating only.

(Either here or lower on the page, you'll want to insert your industry-specific review links)

Google Business Review

Yahoo Local page

These next websites are SUPER IMPORTANT! THANK YOU!

Yelp

Citysearch (and give us a thumbs up)

More sites and things you can do that would be super awesome and appreciated!

Foursquare (share your review as a tip or add your own tip)

Pin us Pinterest.com

Follow us and tweet about us on Twitter.

Facebook! Go to our (your website homepage if you have a Facebook like button on it) and click on the "like" buttons for both the website and go to our (your Facebook page link) and like it as well. Go to our review tab to write a review and to rate us.

Recommend us to your friends or family that also might (want your product x or service y). It is super easy to refer us; just go to our (your website homepage if you have social media buttons on it) and go to the bottom of the page. Use our array of social media tools to share us with your friends. If you know of anyone that needs (product x or service y), please let them know about us. It would be our pleasure to send them free information and a no obligation quote.

Make a short video review and/or actual video (using our product or giving a testimonial) and post it to our (your Facebook page link) and on (your Youtube channel link) and other websites. Be sure to tell us what you did and send us the link(s). Rate and review our videos on our (your Youtube channel link).

Thank you again so much! From all of us at (your business name), thank you for your business, reviews, referrals, and most of all, your passion and enthusiasm for what we do!

Your name

The resources webpage also has links to good and bad examples of review landing webpages.

DO YOU DESERVE AN AWARD?

As you track your great reviews, you'll want to consider emphasizing the websites that will earn you potential customer service awards. You've seen these "Best of" awards, lists, or blog posts haven't you? Many of these awards are given based on getting a certain number of great reviews or votes during the year or a certain time period. I'm not talking about fifty or one hundred reviews either, some only require five to ten great reviews in a year to win an award or designation. No matter what you think of these types of awards, they make for great marketing both on and offline! You can feature an award or designation on your business cards, letterhead, envelopes, sales letters, brochures, website, blog, social media or basically everywhere! You can also issue a news release and get local media attention for your accomplishment. So don't underestimate the marketing power of earning an award or designation.

STOP ARGUING

This was true in the wedding industry and may be true in your industry as well. You could have two groups of business owners in your industry. The first group goes after awards purposely and/or those businesses receive awards because they are at the top in their market. The second group is usually the businesses complaining about these awards being bogus and those are the business owners that are not receiving the awards! Your clients don't know what it took to win or earn that award! You simply played by that organization's or website's rules to "win" or receive a designation. So if you are one of those business owners that think these awards are stupid, either don't go after that award or stop arguing and see them for the marketing value that they really are! Legitimate online reviews are marketing. Legitimate service awards are marketing too.

As I mentioned before, we worked the Fans on Fire system in my wedding DJ company consistently for about five years. Besides gathering hundreds of awesome online reviews, we won eleven state wedding awards. But it even got better! In the first year it was offered, we were inducted into the National Wedding Hall of Fame, a brand new award from TheKnot.com (a major wedding related website). We were one of just 331 of all wedding related companies in the entire United States to receive this award and we were interviewed by two local TV stations. Needless to say, it was great publicity and all because of working the Fans on Fire system and offering great service to our clients! I mention this again not to impress you, but to impress upon you of how impactful the Fans on Fire system can be in your business!

SAMPLE FANS ON FIRE AWARD EMAIL OR LETTER

Want to know how you can do the same? Here is a Fans on Fire letter/ email template that you can use if you are shooting for a specific award:

Dear first name:

Thank you again for (purchasing x product on date/choosing our x service on date, etc) from my company and thank you so much for your positive review and/or comments. It is the highlight of our day to see a great review from one of our satisfied clients!

I know you are busy, but we hope you will take a few moments to review our services on **(specific website).** This will help us to qualify for the **(specific award)**; this will be our third year in a row to qualify if we get enough positive reviews. **THE DEADLINE IS (DATE) AT 12 MIDNIGHT.** If you would, just follow the link below; it's quick, free and easy.

To make it even easier, your written comments are added here if you would like to re-use them: *(Cut and paste your client's review comments here)* (Insert the specific website review link or vote link here.)

Thank you so much for your help! With the current state of the economy, reviews and referrals are more important than ever. Online reviews of (your industry) are very powerful. If you would like to help us even more, please follow the link below:

(Link to your Fans on Fire page on your website)

From all of us at (your company name), thank you again for your business, reviews, referrals, and most of all, your passion and enthusiasm for what we do!

Sincerely,

Your name

Contact information

Your website, social media, etc.

AWARDS AND YOUR UNIQUE SELLING PROPOSITION (USP)

Whatever industry your business is in, search for awards that you might be eligible for. Read the rules carefully and plan to go for it! As I've said about certain industries that are really competitive, you need a number of great reviews just to be on a level playing field with your competition. The same goes for awards! If your biggest competition has won several awards, you better go after those awards or different and better awards so you can be on equal or better footing. I considered these awards so important to our marketing strategies that I incorporated them into our USP. I updated this USP over the years, but before I sold the company it was "Area's Most Awarded DJ's & Uplighting"! Now what client or customer wouldn't want to do business with the "area's most awarded" service or business in your area? I rest my case!

WHEN TO USE MASS EMAIL

I'm going to violate my previous no mass email recommendation now. I have successfully used a mass email campaign to our Fans on Fire database for one specific award or year-end review push. After following this strategy for several years, our database of biggest fans contained hundreds of clients. Which was awesome! January is a big month for wedding DJ sales. So to beef up our review website profiles or to target any last minute award deadlines, I've sent out one or two additional requests for reviews in December. These were successful in getting a few additional reviews, but not many because these fans had already been contacted a number of times. But it was still worth it! A few of these fans would unsubscribe from our list, but that was ok because we typically don't do repeat weddings!

SPECIAL OFFERS!

I am always thinking about the maximum marketing leverage possible when it comes to business and you should be too! For example, you could also include special offers, coupons, and more with each of your Fans on Fire letters and emails. These could be for your client to use or to share with their friends. Who better to send your best specials and promotions to than your biggest fans? Keep in mind that too much promotional material could distract from the original purpose of your client contact, getting those great reviews!

WHAT TO DO WITH OLDER REVIEWS

The more recent the initial review the better, but if you have been collecting reviews already in your business, that's awesome! You may have stacks or years of previous reviews sitting in a file somewhere. You can still go back, even up to several years to leverage those great comments. Just don't do them all at once to the same review website. If your review profile on a website is new or only gets one review on average per month and all of a sudden you receive ten or more reviews in one month, that could be seen as unnatural or spam and get your valuable reviews hidden or removed.

Older reviews are probably less likely to post an online review because of the time that has passed since the client did business with you. But even a lower response rate is still a response! The more memorable your product or service, the better the response rate will be. For example, we had a wedding client post to a review website a full eight months after her wedding! With that in mind, you can probably figure only one in ten of your previous or older happy clients will review you now. Whatever you do, don't miss out on all of the marketing leverage from your previous client's reviews!

WHERE ELSE CAN YOU USE THOSE AWESOME REVIEWS?

This almost goes without saying, but if you have printed marketing material such as brochures, information packets, etc., you can use those great reviews there as well! Printed promotional pieces that get picked up or mailed to potential clients get a real marketing boost when you add reviews. Make sure to incorporate your amazing reviews in that material. For example, when we did a promotional mailing to potential wedding clients, whatever postage weight was left was used with another sheet of happy client reviews. Another tip! Use your most recent reviews on your marketing material! Although I can't remember a client mentioning it, I believe it was more powerful to use client reviews that were only a few weeks to a few months old. What better way to sell your business than a happy customer from just a few short weeks ago raving about you!

Yes, that means we included the date of reviews in our promotional material. In my opinion, so many businesses get lazy with this and make one promotional sales sheet with reviews with no date and use it for five or more years. So it might be a small thing, but which business would you choose? One with pages of happy, recent reviews or a business with one sheet of reviews with no dates? Providing more awesome reviews is always better! Your potential client may not read past the first five of them, but the psychological impact of having a bunch more leaves a big positive impact. This is what I mean by leveraging every marketing dollar out of your happy clients' reviews!

SOCIAL MEDIA, WEBSITE AND BLOGS

You can use great reviews in your social media and on your website and blog. Although I don't recommend it, you can even link an online review profile with reviews directly to your website or you can use an embed code. If you do this, it increases the chances that an upset customer will post to that profile before you've received the initial review from them directly. Another idea would be to have a fan of the week or month post on your social media and on your blog. You could do a blog post with all of your happy client reviews received that month.

Hand written thank you notes from clients also make great content for social media, blogs and websites. Simply take a picture of the thank you note(s) and use them. When reviews are posted on Internet properties that you control like your website, blog, social media, etc., having an image of a handwritten thank you note is even more believable than a text only review. Even better, if you have a picture of your client or you (or your staff) and your client together, post that along with the comment image or text! You can still use or recycle those handwritten thank you comments in your Fans on Fire system.

HIDDEN REVIEWS AND YELP!

Despite your best efforts, some of your online reviews will get hidden or removed. I've had duplicate reviews removed from Google. But these were identical reviews on multiple Google My Business profiles. That being said, in my experience, Yelp is the biggest culprit for hiding online reviews!

Yelp is probably the most hated of online review websites by small businesses. The news is full of lawsuits by businesses trying to fight the way Yelp operates. Don't fight Yelp, use them! After all, a business can sign up for free on Yelp and you don't have to buy their advertising. I never paid for Yelp advertising and as stated before, Yelp was another page one listing for my wedding DJ company on Google.

Yelp may also be the most challenging of online review websites to master. Yelp has this super-secret formula for what reviews they will make public or keep hidden. The filtered or hidden reviews are available through a link at the bottom of your public Yelp profile. At the time of this writing, a potential customer can click on that link and have access to these hidden reviews. However, you cannot see the star rating, only the comments. For example, in my wedding DJ company, we had three public reviews being shown and seven hidden ones. All of the hidden reviews were legitimate of course, but the Yelp filter did not recommend them.

How do you get those filtered or hidden reviews to show up on Yelp? The number one way is to get your customer more involved in other Yelp reviews. Respond to the review, friend your customer on Yelp, like their review and send them a message through Yelp asking them to review other businesses. Yelp is suspicious of reviewers that sign up, leave one review and then never return to the website. Reviews from customers like that will likely be hidden. Hidden reviews can come back to life, show up publicly and then disappear again! So if you have a Yelp profile with reviews now, check it out to see if any great reviews from clients are hidden. If so, try some of these strategies to get them to show up publicly.

Yelp even has a policy against asking for reviews! Yelp is the only review website I know of that has that policy! That's a "policy" that I say you need to bend. In one study of Yelp by the Harvard Business School, an increase of just one star for a restaurant led to a 5 to 9% increase in revenue. So keep working at it. Positive Yelp reviews will pay off for you! See the resources webpage for more tips on filtered reviews in Google and on Yelp.

EMPLOYEES AND REVIEWS

So how can you use reviews when working with your staff? You could offer an incentive to your employees for doing the great work that leads to receiving an awesome review from a customer. For example, you could offer your employees a monetary incentive or a gift for taking care of a client in an exceptional way. Have your employees remind clients that a feedback form will be coming and that their manager would appreciate hearing how they did. For example, at the end of every phone call I make to my web hosting company's support line, I get read a script by the technician reminding me to watch for an email from their manager asking for feedback. And it works; of the few reviews I leave personally, this was one of them!

In my wedding DJ company, our initial review form sent to clients was coded for the particular DJ that performed at a reception. This was great immediate feedback for how a particular DJ was serving our clients. We were able to share both positive and constructive feedback received from clients with their individual DJ. This helped us to know what areas of a DJ's performance deserved praise and where they needed coaching. If you have a staff, your business should incorporate a similar system. Although certain aspects of your company's service cannot be narrowed down to the responsibility of a single staff member. Many points of contact with your customer *can* be traced to an individual employee, their job duties or their team. Then, you can offer praise to particular employees or the team that helped generate great reviews. You can develop an employee of the month program or a number of other reward or bonus programs for top staff. By presenting these awards in company meetings, it further encourages other staff members to strive toward higher customer satisfaction.

Train your staff to watch for Fans on Fire in the moment and/or video and picture opportunities! If your employees are interacting with a happy customer, have them get a picture or a fun video testimonial! A video could last a few seconds to a few minutes. Don't worry about how professional it looks; if the camera shakes, or if the sound isn't perfect, that's no problem. You want real, authentic, customer feedback that you can use on YouTube or in a promotional video for your business. You can further incentivize an employee to get video testimonials. Featuring testimonial videos on your website, blog and social media is very powerful. If the customer isn't comfortable doing a video, ask to take a photo with them. A picture of the customer next to their positive review puts that review on steroids!

Here's another important area but it is one of my least favorite! You can use feedback from clients to help determine the future of a particular staff member. I know this is a touchy subject and many business owners feel a deep loyalty to their staff members. Believe me, I know how hard it is to separate your personal relationship from your business relationship with staff members. Early on and, unfortunately, even in later years, I continued to work with disc jockeys that had gotten some negative feedback on the initial review. I believed that we could train, coach, "fix" a particular DJ and their performance issues. Some were coachable and started receiving great feedback from their clients and some were not. One of my big lessons was realizing that continuing to use a staff member that performed poorly helps no one, not even the staff member! You ultimately will have to figure out at what point a staff member's contribution is costing your company too much. Just consider this: continuing to work with someone that causes complaints is not only bad for your company, but it's also bad for that individual. The faster you part ways, the faster that person can be on to another work or job opportunity that could be a better fit.

Important – Change Will Happen!

I have purposely kept my strategies somewhat flexible in nature because of the huge variety of review websites out there. My strategies should work with most of them. However, you may have to make adjustments for a few of them depending on their rules. Some websites may have rules or guidelines that don't mesh exactly with what I'm recommending. So do some additional research if you are concerned about using a particular strategy. It is your responsibility to choose the right review strategy for your business. You can stay up-to-date with changes in the online review industry by signing up for my email list and bonus templates (tomkenemore.com/firebonuses).

Conclusion to Leveraging Great Reviews and Actions

In this chapter you learned a bunch of additional strategies in the Fans on Fire review system! You learned how to design your Fans on Fire webpage and how to compete for customer service awards in your industry. I also covered many more ways you can leverage your great customer reviews including working with your employees. Your next action for this chapter is to create your Fans on Fire webpage and include that link in all of your contacts with your fans. I would love to know what your biggest takeaway is from these last few chapters! Please take a quick moment to email me directly (tk@tomkenemore.com), thanks so much! Get all of my bonus content for this chapter and the book (tomkenemore.com/firebonuses). Then in the next chapter we will wrap up this book by discussing how to handle negative and fake reviews.

Chapter 7

Reducing the Impact of Negative and Fake Reviews

"Your most unhappy customers are your greatest source of learning."

– Bill Gates

INTRODUCTION

On the flip side of leveraging your great reviews is minimizing the impact of negative and fake online reviews. Why is this so important? Studies show that negative reviews have a big impact on a potential customer in choosing who to buy from. In a recent BrightLocal Consumer Review Survey, only 13% of consumers would consider using a business that has a one or two-star rating. Even a three-star rating got only 57% of consumers to do business with them, leaving 43% of consumers to keep looking! That's leaving a lot of business on the table for your competition! So in this chapter we are going to discuss strategies on how to handle negative and fake online reviews. As I mentioned earlier, if you have a quality product or service, you shouldn't get many negative reviews.

YOU WILL GET A NEGATIVE ONLINE REVIEW

If you are in business long enough, you will eventually get a negative online review and possibly more than one. Rather than cursing about it or ignoring it, what can you do? Well one of the big reasons for leveraging your awesome reviews is so that the occasional negative review that slips through your Fans on Fire system will get buried online! In fact, your awesome five-star online reviews will seem more believable if there are a few three and four-star reviews mixed in. It looks suspicious to have 50 five-star reviews on one website with no one to four-star reviews. One or two negative reviews won't affect your average rating that much if you have a lot of positive ones, and some industry review websites will push your lower reviews to the bottom of the list, further reducing their potential damage.

Remember to respond as positively as you can to a negative online review. You can drastically reduce the impact with a thoughtful, heartfelt, personal response and by describing how you intend for your business to do better in the future. Offer to make it right with the customer and request that they contact you.

If you recognize or can research the customer's name, username or email, be sure to follow up with them in private to see what you can do to correct the complaint. This is best done with a phone call if you have their number. If you can satisfy your customer's complaint, ask them to go back and edit their review to reflect the improvement. Many review websites will allow edits and changes to a previously posted review. Be authentic with your client, but tread lightly. Let them know a poor review hurts your business and your employees and frankly you and your family! Depending on your business and the circumstances around the complaint, asking your customer to change their review could backfire on you and possibly make it worse. So weigh the pros and cons.

CATCH A COMPLAINT BEFORE THEY COMPLAIN ONLINE

The key is to catch a complaining customer before they post a negative review online. If you followed my suggestions back in the initial review process, you should receive the review from a customer directly. If you receive a negative review at the initial review point, that is great! What! Yes, that's great! As Bill Gates once said "*Your most unhappy customers are your greatest source of learning.*" A complaining customer at this point is super valuable feedback for you and your team plus that customer likely has not spread their negative review around the Internet yet. But you don't have a lot of time. Depending on how bad the comments are and how much contact information you have for the customer, you'll need to decide what to do. If the complaint is minor or just constructive feedback, you may choose to use the information internally to improve your business. You'll want to at least thank the customer for their feedback. In the bonus downloadable

PDF package, there is a template for a "Response to a negative review or feedback."

SAMPLE RESPONSE TO NEGATIVE FEEDBACK

Here is that sample text for use in replying to negative feedback, or you can edit with your own words. I recommend using this only if the rating received is one or two stars or has lots of negative comments. Be sure to remove my notes before sending to your client.

Dear Customer/Client first name

Thank you for taking time to give us feedback regarding your recent purchase (of x product/y service). I am very sorry to hear that you were disappointed with us (or the product or service). I will personally bring up your comments with the staff member you worked with (or the person that handles that part of the product/service) and discuss your concerns.

Although concerns about our (products/service) are rare, we take them very seriously. We work hard to please our customers, and therefore feedback is very important to us. We are always striving to improve as a company and individually.

(If you will be offering them some kind of refund, I would put that here, for example: I would like to offer you (or as we discussed on the phone) (a full/partial refund, a $xx gift certificate toward your next purchase, a replacement of product x/service y,) or whatever you want to offer).

Again, thank you so much for your comments. (And if you want to add: I hope you will visit us again soon!)

Sincerely,

Your personal name, title (NO review site links here; you don't want them sharing their experience . . . too risky)

CONTACT SERIOUS COMPLAINTS IMMEDIATELY!

If you receive a more serious complaint from a customer, you'll want to contact them right away with a phone call. And no, not later that day – an immediate phone call! Your customer is probably not expecting to be contacted by you so quickly; that alone will help them to realize you care about their concerns. This is where you put on your humble hat and just listen. Don't make excuses; own the problem, even if it's not your fault! Your customer is dying to do business with a company that owns their mistakes, even if it's not directly your fault. Maybe your shipment of product arrived late due to a problem with your shipping company. Maybe a product you are reselling didn't live up to your customer's expectations. Whatever the problem, ask your customer, "What can we do to make this right?" Oftentimes, customers just want to be heard and will be satisfied with a phone call from you and an apology.

I know how hard this is to do. Imagine getting a long complaint letter back from a client saying your company ruined their wedding! The biggest day of their life and it can't be redone! The memories of receiving these kinds of letters still haunts me! This was the toughest part of running my wedding DJ company. Right or wrong, I took this feedback personally.

I know how easy it is to keep putting this off and to put it at the bottom of the to do list. The longer you procrastinate on contacting your customer, the harder it will feel like when you actually do it. Plus small complaints from customers can turn into big ones when not handled quickly, personally and professionally.

DO AS MUCH AS YOU CAN AFFORD TO PLEASE YOUR CUSTOMER

If a simple phone call and apology still wasn't enough, here are some other possible solutions (depending on your industry, price point and what you can afford to do):

- Full or partial refund
- If appropriate, redo the service or replace the product
- Provide a discount or credit toward future purchase from your company

- Give them something of value from another business, a gift or gift certificate to a restaurant, hotel, etc.

- With all of the above, include a heartfelt apology letter similar to our previous example

Offer as much satisfaction as your budget allows to a complaining client. Offer more than expected if you can, even a combination of the solutions above.

Here is a bad situation turned into positive experience to demonstrate what I'm talking about from a national chain hotel on Virginia Beach. The first night in the hotel was rotten! The room was acceptable, but the hotel guest above us decided to go bowling in their room throughout the night (or at least it sounded that way). I called the front desk to report it in the middle of the night and they said they would send security to check it out. However, the noise continued intermittently throughout the rest of the night. To make this story short, I complained in the morning about the excessive noise through the night and a bad night's sleep. Of course it wasn't directly the hotel's fault, but it was the hotel's responsibility to make me happy. So without much complaining the next morning, the hotel was quick to offer a free upgrade to an ocean side, king room and a free additional night's stay. This was a lot more than I expected. The hotel went above and beyond to make me happy. So what did I do? I posted it on my personal Facebook profile where hundreds of my friends saw it and got a positive impression of this hotel brand. Plus, if the hotel had asked me for feedback on my experience, I would have written a glowing review!

DON'T OFFER TOO LITTLE

If you offer too little to a complaint, you risk upsetting an unhappy customer even more. Pay particular attention to a customer that makes a reference to commenting or sharing online about how bad your service or product was. Remember, one bad review spread around the Internet could be out there forever, and cost you far more over the years in lost business. If, despite your efforts, some bad reviews get onto your review websites, at least your unhappy client should mention that you attempted to make it right. That should help. If your client does not mention the things you did to make it right, then be sure to add those items to your response to the review if allowed on that review website. Most of your potential customers expect you to receive some complaints; they just want to know that on the few complaints you've had, you made it right or attempted to make it right with the customer. Most customers understand that there are some fellow customers that can't be pleased no matter what you do.

MY COMPLAINT EXPERIENCE

Take it from me and my experience owning a wedding DJ company. I think the wedding industry is a challenging one as far as always pleasing your clients. Offering a personal service to couples on the biggest day of their lives can create some big wins and some big disappointments. It was a big stress for my staff and I to make sure every client was happy with their DJ and our service. Our challenge was made even larger by the fact that we performed at hundreds of weddings every year. At any given wedding, there were hundreds of guests who could write us a positive or a negative review. I'll admit in our earlier years of operation, our quality suffered. Our fast growth of doubling in size for four straight years led to some tough training and staffing issues. However, as we matured as a company and began to focus on higher quality service, our complaints were greatly reduced. Of the few complaints received in our later years, we listened and refunded as much as necessary to keep a client from being tempted to write a negative review on one of our online review profiles. In recent years, I can think of only one client that left a negative online review after receiving a refund. Thankfully, that terrible review was buried by many, many amazing reviews by happy wedding clients! By actively working the Fans on Fire system, your awesome online reviews will bury the few negative ones you may get.

ALWAYS DISPUTE FAKE REVIEWS

Yes, unfortunately, there are fake online reviews and they can be a challenge, if not impossible to get rid of. For example, going back to my wedding DJ company. Before Google My Business Pages, you may remember there was Google Places. If you were in the phone book, you got an automatic Google Place page. Well, before I started actively using that profile, a Google user gave us a one-star rating. And to make it more challenging, about six months later the same user gave us another one-star rating. At the time, you were able to see the user's username and other reviews they had posted. So I did a little research on the reviewer. This user had rated about twenty different DJ companies and hundreds of other businesses. They had given a whole string of either one-star or five-star ratings. Now there is almost no way that this user could have been a client of twenty different DJ companies. So I marked those reviews as spam and contacted Google asking to have them removed. Guess what, nothing happened. A few months later, I marked those one-star reviews as spam again and contacted Google again, and still no response. By the time Google Places was upgraded to Google Plus pages (then Google My Business) I was starting to get concerned about the fake reviews. We only had the two one-star ratings on the profile at the time; it was a pretty sad profile to say the least. But I worked the Fans on Fire system and now the company has a 4.5-star rating and those one-star reviews are buried at the bottom!

HOW SHOULD YOU COMMENT ON A FAKE REVIEW?

Here was my response to the fake one-star reviews on my wedding DJ company's Google My Business profile:

"This is a spam review. Google has done several updates to their reviews and how they show up over the years. So now the older reviews no longer show a user name. However, several years ago when you could see the user's name, this user gave us a one-star rating twice with no comments. At the time, you were able to click on the user name to see other reviews that the user had posted. This user had given out hundreds of reviews and many of them to other DJ companies, also giving them low marks. So please disregard this review and look at our most recent reviews written by real people and real events. Thank You! Tom Kenemore, CEO"

So again, don't ignore fake reviews. Dispute them with the online review website and comment on them. The fake reviews may not get taken down, but at least if you comment on them, it will show that you care about your reputation. There is a good chance that potential customers will believe your side of the story and still want to do business with you. Even though fake negative reviews can make you the angriest, respond only after you've cooled down with a straightforward, positive and authentic comment.

CONCLUSION AND ACTIONS ON HOW TO HANDLE NEGATIVE AND FAKE REVIEWS

In this chapter we discussed the ugly side of the review process, how to handle negative and fake reviews. It may not be fun, but this part of the Fans on Fire system is essential. You learned how to minimize the impact that negative and fake reviews could have on your business. So for your last action steps for this book, do that dreaded search again. Type the name of your business followed by review(s). Do you have any negative or fake reviews posted about your business? Your next action step is to respond to them appropriately using the tools and suggestions from this chapter. Be sure to get all of my bonus content for this chapter and the book now (tomkenemore.com/firebonuses).

CONCLUSION

Congratulations on finishing this book and learning how the Fans on Fire system can benefit your business! I covered many aspects of the online review process. You learned what online review websites are and how important they are to your business. You also learned how to start getting reviews from your clients and how to leverage them for maximum benefit. I also covered the dark side of reviews and gave you some tips on handling negative and fake reviews. Now you are ready to leverage your happy customers' reviews into free marketing dollars for your business. Remember to work this program regularly for maximum benefit for your business. So if you haven't started implementing the action steps, start now! You can always look back on a chapter when you need tips on handling a particular review situation. "Whatever you do, don't stop asking for reviews once you've started," says Mike Blumenthal, a review industry expert. "The reality is that you don't need ten reviews a week . . . In fact, you don't need ten reviews a month or a quarter there to succeed. Most businesses need to accrue one review every month or two so that at the end of 3 years you will have 30." If you haven't emailed me already, I would love to hear what your key takeaway is from reading this book! Please email me (tk@tomkenemore.com) what your biggest aha was!

Brian Klemmer, one of my mentors would say this quote from Ken Blanchard all the time, "Feedback is the breakfast of champions," and that goes both ways! If you have suggestions on improvements, questions or would like to see more added to the book, please email me as well.

Now that you have finished this book, you'll never guess what I'm going to ask you for! Haha! But seriously, please write a review on what you thought about the book and how the strategies have benefited your business. You can find the review link here (tomkenemore.com/firereview) or by going back to the Amazon website and going to this book's sales page. Your review, as you've just learned is very important to me! Your review will help other entrepreneurs and small business owners find this book in the crowded book marketplace. Help me to reach more business owners like yourself so they can benefit from the Fans on Fire system. Does your association or business need a speaker or consultant on this topic? Just contact me below for speaking and consulting options! I invite you to share this book with your colleagues as well as through social media, business groups or however you see fit. Speaking of social media, feel free to connect with me though all of my social media profiles below! I look forward to connecting with you, discussing and brainstorming on the latest online review strategies, marketing ideas and other small business interests! I truly appreciate you and your passion for my work! Good luck to you and all of the future business success you will create!

Tom Kenemore

Speaking and Consulting Services

Need a speaker for your next conference or association meeting? Contact me below to have me speak live at your event about Online Review Marketing. Additional topics on entrepreneurship, small business and marketing are available. Need help setting up your online review marketing system? Contact me about direct consulting for your specific industry or business. My contact information is in the next section.

Connect with Me

Connect with me on social media to get the most up-to-date small business and entrepreneurship content that I'm sharing!

Join my email list and get all bonus email, letter and website templates!

(tomkenemore.com/firebonuses)

For speaking and consulting, contact me through Lake Effect Media

(218-485-4252)

Email me

(tk@tomkenemore.com)

My website

(tomkenemore.com)

Google Plus

(plus.google.com/+TomKenemore)

Like my Facebook page

(www.facebook.com/tomkenemore)

Follow me on Twitter

(twitter.com/Tom_Kenemore)

Subscribe to my Youtube Channel

(www.youtube.com/user/TomKenemore)

Connect with me on Linkedin

(www.linkedin.com/in/tomkenemore)

Special Offer On The Companion Online Course

This book's companion online course and my best selling course! *Google, Facebook & Yelp – Online Review Marketing for Entrepreneurs*!

You and your friends can enroll for a special low rate, just $10! (tomkenemore.com/reviewscourse)

JOIN OVER 5400 SUCCESSFUL STUDENTS!! 24+ 5 star reviews!

Why take the online companion course after reading this book?

- You get to hear (and see) me deliver the content! Reinforce your understanding of the strategies.

- Participate in discussions with other students.

- Ask me questions, I'll respond and/or create additional sections of the course based on your questions.

- Bonus content not covered in the book and more bonus templates!

- This course is divided into short sections that you can take on your own time whenever you have a few moments. This course is built on the world-renowned Udemy platform with millions of students! You can even download the smartphone app and take the course on the road wherever you are! Plus you get lifetime access and free access to updates to the course!

- You won't risk a cent. The course comes with Udemy's unconditional thirty-day money back guarantee. So if you find that the course doesn't meet your needs, just say so and we will refund your money immediately. It's easy, no hoops to jump through and no hard feelings.

More Online Courses By Tom Kenemore

One last thing! I just wanted to share a couple other courses with you and your friends!

Entrepreneurs Guide To Finance Your Business or Startup! Finance your business or startup now! Over 30 ways to get the cash you need from an entrepreneur who raised over $300,000!

You and your friends can enroll for a special low rate, just $10!

(tomkenemore.com/financecourse)

JOIN OVER 1600 STUDENTS!! – 9+ 5 STAR REVIEWS!

Entrepreneurship 101—How To Start A Business You Love Now! Stuck on what business idea to start? Match your skills, personality, passions and more to the right business for you!

You and your friends can enroll for a special low rate, just $10!

(tomkenemore.com/startupcourse)

JOIN OVER 3800 STUDENTS!! – 19+ 5 STAR REVIEWS!

About the Author

So who am I? I've always been an entrepreneur! At 15, I took over my first "real" small business, a bee swarm removal service from one of my uncles. This was before I could even drive a car! In college, I took $600 in "leftover" student financial aid money and a Sear's credit card and started a mobile DJ company. After graduation and after more than a dozen job rejections, I took that little DJ company and turned it into one of the largest DJ entertainment services in the Upper Midwest.

So far I've started and owned six small businesses and sold millions of dollars in products and services. That's over 25 years of small business experience, and I've never had more than a summer job for regular employment!

Later my wedding DJ company was inducted as a national wedding industry hall of fame honoree by The Knot Wedding Network! We also won 11 state wedding awards and received a lot of local media attention . . . all because of great customer service, receiving positive reviews and leveraging them to the max! I've since sold that company so I could focus on helping entrepreneurs and small business owners like you! Today my passion is training and education in entrepreneurship, small business and marketing topics. I also enjoy speaking to groups of high school and college students about taking the entrepreneurial path rather than traditional employment.

www.ingramcontent.com/pod-product-compliance
Lightning Source LLC
Chambersburg PA
CBHW060410190526
45169CB00002B/834